The Warrior Wife

The Warrior Wife

She Marches with Lord Sabaoth, God Of Angel Armies,
and Takes Territory from Hell.

LaDeidre Maris

The Warrior Wife

Published by Living Water Book,

Christian Division of Butterfly Typeface Publishing House,

Little Rock, Arkansas 72201

ISBN 978-1-7357073-7-2

Living Water Books

John 7:38
He who believes in me, as the scripture has said,
Out of his heart will flow rivers of living water.

Dedication

I am my beloved, and my beloved is mine

Song of Solomon 6:3

This book is dedicated to

the love of my life Charles Maris.

I will never ever stop interceding on your behalf. The alliance I have with God surrounds us with the Angelic Host. We are guarded and protected by the Glory of God.

Table of Contents

The Warrior Wife & Her Armor

The Warrior Wife & Her Husband

The Weaponized Voice

An Impartation from God (Psalm 29)

*Lord, I depend on your strengthening love to breathe on my sound and give me range in the realm of the spirit. I declare that my husband is an **InTune Husband,** Intune with you concerning my heart. I am a **Warrior Wife,** the dwelling place Of God; skilled to hear, influence, and protect my husband's heart as God instructs. My voice is my weapon, and I refuse to wound him with the sound you entrust within me. Lord, heighten my sensitivity to the spirit realm to pray against seen and unseen attacks that desire to go toe to toe with me. The adversary wants my sound, but my mouth belongs to you, God.*

I submit my voice to your sound that Psalms 29 teaches us about. Your voice through me is full of majesty, and it hovers over many waters. I am gentle and royal. Your voice through me breaks the cedar of Lebanon into pieces and shakes the wilderness. I am a force that the enemy cannot stop. Your voice through me divides the flames of fire, like lightning you and I strike when we speak. I am the blazing fire that purifies the atmosphere of my home. Your voice through me makes even the deer give birth. I am a life-giver and healer. Your voice through me performs miracles as we transform the dead, dry bones (situation) into the living. You are my Lord and lover. All that I am and what I can do, hinges on who you are. I am you, and you are me. When fear approaches me, your fearless perfect love shields me. Your love defines me, and I can face tomorrow because of my faith in you. Your love prepares me to suit up in the full armor of you, God. I am your voice through movement.

This is not a letter to be taken lightly; instead, it is a declaration placed within me, sealed in the blood of Christ, and written out.

Signed,

The Warrior Wife, LaDeidre Maris

Preface

I imagine a conversation occurred in Heaven between God and satan (like the Book of Job) where the adversary asked our Lord for permission to strike and sift us as wheat. In Luke 22:31-32, satan requests to sift Peter like wheat, but the Lord tells Peter, I have prayed for you that your faith will not fail. The amplified version of this scripture says satan demanded permission. He demanded permission in the courts of Heaven to sift us as wheat; to sift means to examine and separate. Sifting someone as wheat in spirit is intended to beat them up, separate them from Christ, torment them, wear them out, break them down in hopes of causing the person to self-destruct.

- How do you combat this when the enemy is trying to sift the entire family as wheat?
- How do you fight when you are trying to heal but you are deeply wounded?

I need to be completely honest with you; before God taught me, I did not know how to fight in faith. I cursed and fought in the world for two reasons, and they are as follows:

1.) If I were picked on and cornered with no way out, or

2.) If anyone threatened the life of those I loved.

I soon found out that fighting in the Kingdom of God with wisdom is different from fighting in the world with foolishness. I needed training and transformation. God said, "Keep your reasons for fighting because I too am passionate about those I love. I will use this for my glory, but I need your mind renewed."

CHAPTER ONE

The Warrior Wife
FIND HER

You are my war club, my weapon for battle — with you, I shatter nations, with you, I destroy kingdoms Jeremiah 51:20.

Find The Warrior

Hiding in the Shadow of The Almighty

Who is she?

What is her value?

Where is she?

Who sent her?

The Warrior Wife is the Bride of Christ. We hear this so much that it gets downplayed and becomes a phrase that Christians use. However, our power lies in the knowledge and revelation of this truth. The Warrior Wife knows the death, burial, and resurrection of Christ. She is the church for which he sacrificed himself; this is personal. She was named successor and given the title victor. She is not a building in which people go to fellowship. She is the essence and mentality of Christ. According to Ephesians 5:25. He gave himself up for her. She is the expression of God's heart in the earth, which is why He can draw her husband closer to Him through her. 1 Peter 3:1.

The husband draws closer to God just by encountering her godly character and obedience to God.

What is her value?

She is the most prominent and influential woman you have ever known, not because everyone in the land knows her but because of God surrounding her, Christ seated with her, The Holy Spirit within her, and Heaven as her audience. She is a well-known powerhouse. The wedding invitations for the bridegroom and his bride went out before the foundations of the world. Heaven threw the engagement party, and the angels witnessed the wedding of Christ to his bride long before we ever stepped foot on earth. If you have not noticed, I am talking about you, Warrior Wife, but I will finish sharing this truth until it becomes your reality; then, I will switch my verbiage from using (she) to using terms such as (You and I.) I know you think that only your enemies discuss you, but you are mistaken. Heaven has open discussions about how to assist you with all your endeavors in the land.

God sent angels to minister to you and help fulfill the purpose planted within you by Christ. Angelic beings travel around the globe, helping you to dismantle evil plots and establish connections that you will need at different junctions of your life. The warrior wife is well known, and she is so powerful that it supersedes her comprehension. I know what you are thinking…...

You are looking at your current situation, home, or place of brokenness, and you are judging your power based upon what you see happening in the natural. 2 Corinthians 12:9-11 states God's grace is sufficient, and His power is made perfect in weakness. Therefore, let us boast about our weaknesses so that Christ's power may rest on us. This scripture gives us a new set of eyes to see the power of God resting upon us in our weaknesses despite what challenges arise. Faith is the eyesight that reaches into the realm of the spirit, grabs the impossible, and says, now manifest. Do not let your natural senses or environment deceive you into thinking that you are a nobody with little to no means. When God describes his covenant relationship with you, he says Ezekiel 16:8, I gave you my solemn oath and entered a covenant with you, and you became mine declares the Sovereign Lord.

Where Is She?

She is hidden in Christ, assuming her position. In that position, God is entirely responsible. Even when things appear challenging, we can stake our entire life on the fact that God is omnipresent and omnipotent. (He is everywhere and all-powerful.) It is ok to repeat that. Just say God is responsible for me. I belong to Him, and I am in covenant with Him. Covenant means a legally binding agreement that cannot be revoked. In other words, God will not cancel the partnership and relationship with you like others have in your life. He will not walk away from you, which is why he promises never to leave or forsake you. In the courts of Heaven, the paperwork has been signed and sealed by the blood of the lamb. So, let us establish right now within our hearts and minds that we are the Bride of Christ.

THIS IS OUR TRUTH. OWN IT

We are seated in heavenly places, whether at home, the spa, taking care of our husbands, working, grocery shopping, exercising, or nurturing the children. We are still seated in Heaven because God lives within us. The warrior wife is vital, and her existence dances through history. She has the heart posture of John 14:11, Believe me, when I say, I am in the father and the father is in me. Believe on account of the works themselves. This is a mindset that takes on the mantle of marriage. Many marry without understanding the mindset of Christ in marriage, and without this understanding, roles are reversed. Husbands expect the wives to do everything while they do nothing, or wives may expect husbands to do everything while having limited knowledge of what is required of them. Somehow the requirements have become limited to natural abilities such as cooking, sex, taking care of kids, and making money. While these are essential in marriage, our power and authority go far beyond those natural needs. Think about it?

If marriage were limited to everything I just named, it would be no different from any other role, including the life of a single parent or a caregiver.

My husband and I both have been single parents, so I speak from experience, not from a place of judgment. Marriage is more than cooking, cleaning, making money, having sex, and raising children. Do not allow anyone to minimize your God-given role. Marriage begins in spirit, first, where two are tightly knitted together as one. You are a first responder. You can feel and sense not only the heart of your husband, but you can discern his movement, cover him, and usher him into the presence of God. Galatians 5:16 tells us to walk in the spirit. Elisha told his armor-bearer Gehazi (did not my heart go with you), 2 Kings 5:26. There's so much we can accomplish in spirit. Elisha gave insight into discerning the movement of his servant in spirit. He knew what was occurring and when he became filled with evil intent.

Who Sent Her?

The Warrior Wife and Christ have a sacred bond, sealed by his blood, and His blood courses through her veins. He reveals truths to her. She knows her groom will one day return for her, so her role here on earth is essential beyond rubies' value. Jesus is the lover of her soul; her imprint in others' lives is one of significant impact because she unveils the truth of God in the lives of those assigned to her. The Warrior Wife takes that mentality of speaking biblical principles and allows the word of God to build her and others.

The word of God impregnates her, and everyone she connects with breaks forth with this light. Just a reminder, I am talking about you! My husband has this scripture he prays over us; Galatians 4:19, I travail in birth concerning you again until Christ be fully developed in you, some versions say until Christ be fully formed in you. While Christ and The Warrior Wife are one, she is in her maturation process on earth to become who God ordained her to be in spirit, which is why life presents obstacles. Obstacles are nothing more than opportunities to unleash God on them. She is humble, bold, and courageous as a lion yet meek and gentle as a lamb. She is the lion and the lamb because that's who Christ is, according to Revelations 5:5-6. The Warrior Wife has this authoritative presence about her that leads people to Christ by her behavior.

The Warrior Wife

- Who is she? (This is who you are)

- Where is she? (Hiding within you)

- Who sent her into the earth? (God sent you, and no devil from Hell can stop you.)

You are not a mistake. you were in Heaven with him, and he saw a need for you right next to your husband.) He made you and helped you. Do not be afraid Isaiah 44:2. You possess more than you can ever hope, think, or imagine. Heaven is at your fingertips.

You are not a wife by accident. (Romans 8:28) You were a bride before you became a natural wife. Your marriage into Heaven with the Lord of Host qualifies you for battle. God assigned angels to you but what usually happens is we determine our wins based upon ourselves. When we notice our weaknesses, we lose hope. Let's suit up and address your armor.

CHAPTER TWO

Welcome to Basic Training for The Special Ops Forces

A time to love, and a time to hate, a time of war, and a time of peace

Ecclesiastes 3:8.

Warrior Wife

Welcome to Basic Training for
The Special Ops Forces

1st, God calls us into him, and under his tutelage, we are precise and direct. We know the location of our adversary because we sense him moving. The Holy Spirit is our alarm system, and our discernment is keen. (Welcome to class!)

2nd God calls on us when a plan of attack has already been devised against our husbands' because we are the secret weapons to catch the enemy off guard while he is preoccupied with the initial plan. As we move in sync with the Holy Spirit, we are the reinforcement for our home. Our weapons are like silent missiles. (Welcome to class!)

3rd And Lastly, God calls on us to clean the camp and receive the blessing because our prayers sweep the territory. Our worship and prayers remain in the cracks of our homes as a seal so that it isn't penetrable. We've been enlisted by Lord Sabaoth, The God of Angel Armies. Suit up it is time to wage war. (Welcome to class!)

Special Forces Basic Training

Ascension In Spirit Requires Obedience on Earth.

It was a day among days in the year of 2017; I was in our kitchen preparing our younger son's favorite birthday meal, which is mash potatoes and meatloaf. We were all together preparing to celebrate our son's birthday. The loving laughter filled the rooms of our home as our sons played downstairs. The smell of chocolate cake batter lingered in the air. Oh boy, it smelled like happiness.

There was a knock at the door, and I rushed to it because someone was pounding so loud. As I opened the door, I saw two police officers naturally, but spiritually I saw demons behind them. I didn't have enough time to entertain what my eyes saw in the spirit because the officers immediately requested our son. I was confused because he was only six years old. They kept asking for him. I said, officer, why are you here? They served me with papers from a prosecuting attorney's office saying my Husband and I had been accused of child abuse, sexual misconduct, negligence, etc.

28

There were falsified documents, pictures submitted by someone accusing us. I read the papers, but I was gasping for air because I couldn't wrap my mind around this. I kept thinking, this is my baby, whom I love. I was in labor for 19 hours. I carried him in my womb then birthed him out.

I wouldn't dare do anything to hurt him, don't play with me about my son. My thoughts were racing so rapidly because I was the stable and consistent parent he knew before my husband, Charles, entered his life. I would never do anything nor let anyone hurt my baby. Somebody needed to make this clear because the tears from my eyes were dripping onto the paper, and I was in complete disarray. Finally, one of the officers said, "Ma'am, your ex-husband pressed charges against you. We need you to step aside and let us into your home. We must take your son to his dad." I turned around, raced inside of our home, and grabbed my baby. I took him to his room, and I held him. I squeezed him, trying to squeeze every ounce of love I had within me into him. I did not want to let him go. The officers were nonchalant, not compassionate at all. They gave me a couple of minutes to gather his things.

My son had no idea what was going on; he just saw his mom crying and felt the police officers pulling him away. My husband had not arrived from work to even know what was taking place, but it was a direct attack against all of us. One of the officers turned around; as they walked out the door, his demeanor changed. He looked at me and said, "Ma'am, FIGHT!! You seem like a good mother. FIGHT THIS!!

Face to Face with Reality

I felt God. That was a direct charge from Heaven that my spirit captured, but I was too wounded to stand. I fell backward. No, literally, I fell backward. I collapsed, and our oldest son caught me. I cried in his arms like an infant screaming. I lost my breath. Our next to oldest contacted his dad (my husband), and he rushed home. My mother-in-love rushed over, our pastor called, but I was void of any feelings. My husband had called some heavy hitters in our circle to help pray and comfort us, but I was numb. I had no desire to talk, eat or sleep. I couldn't grieve appropriately without thinking of my husband's heart. He was battling this attack differently than myself.

We had no words to pray, no wisdom to say, and no counsel to give ourselves. I had nothing to give my husband.

I screamed, God!! How do I fix this?

What do you want from me, God? What did I do? Please talk to me. Lord, how can I help myself, my husband, and my son all at the same time legally while shutting satan down spiritually? I didn't get a quick answer. I began weeping, worshipping, travailing, speaking in tongues because my mind was starting to entertain the what-if questions. The what if I never get my son back kind of questions. We are innocent, but what if I lose my son for the rest of his life? What if these false allegations stand in court? I pleaded with God to help my unbelief.

Prayer to God

I said, "God, you know me. You know when I sit down and when I rise. You know my every thought better than I do. You know me. You mean to tell me you're just going to let satan come in my home, take my child, accuse my husband and me, then leave our other sons broken. Wait a minute, God!

Please show me something, tell me something." My house was in complete chaos, yet it was in divine order. I don't know about you, but divine order in my life hasn't been perfect. Divine order does not look pretty when it is aligning us for God's purpose. I stretched out in the middle of the floor. While seeking God, I fell into this trance. My body ascended upward in spirit, and He introduced me to someone...

- I knew God from my mother - Alpha and Omega.
- I knew God as my provider – Jehovah Jireh
- I knew God as my savior - Yahweh
- I knew God as my husband and 1st love - Adonai
- I knew God as mighty in my life – Jehovah Gibbor
- I did not know The God of Angel Armies - Lord Sabaoth.
- I did not know God, My Great Judge Jehovah Shaphat (operating in natural and heavenly courtrooms.)

God introduced himself to me and said, "I needed to bring you into my presence, so you'd discover who you are by knowing more about me. I orchestrated this visitation in response to your question. I need you to know me and understand what is at your disposal."

In the vision, God ushered me into the Courts of Heaven and showed me the accusations of satan. I could see these seeds leave a pair of lips and form into words that entered the life of my husband. Everyone working against us in the natural had a different face, but it was satan behind them and through them. Satan was using an earthly vessel to do his dirty work against us, all while trying to confuse our children. I cried even in spirit. I could tell the Holy Spirit within me was grieved because I couldn't stop weeping. I just couldn't grasp the severity of the attacks. God then showed me my husband bent over with daggers penetrating him. That attack in the spirit was the attack pending on earth. I was so furious because satan threatened those whom I love. I asked the spirit of the Lord, "May I intervene? How do I remove the daggers? Lord, Everyone says just pray, but there must be more.

- What do I pray specifically?
- How do I fight?
- I want the intimacy in you, Lord,
- I want the mysteries of The Courts of Heaven,

- I want the conduct and posture of a warrior coated with beauty and grace.
- I want the Holy Spirit to govern my actions.
- I want to see the unseen and address it.

May I step into your authority and protect him. He is your son, and I love him. I want to fight but not the way I use to in the world. The spirit of the Lord spoke, and it was like this mighty rushing water. God said, "I've been waiting on you to approach me for this mantle. This is who you really are. You have legal rights, just as I told Gideon in Judges 6. It's in your bloodline. You are 2nd in command regarding your husband. Let me teach you how to fight. I will train you in spirit and by experiences. Psalm 144:1 Blessed be the Lord, my rock, who trains my hands for war, and my fingers for battle.

LaDeidre, access granted by the blood of the lamb, You have the authority to combat any force. I entered the courts of Heaven, and I petitioned the courts day and night to cease matters that were naturally unfolding. Spiritually, I was bombarding Heaven, and I could not afford to stop praying.

Thy Kingdom Come Thy Will Be Done On earth

Naturally, I was meeting with attorneys, investigators, and detectives. Just as I was finding out my legal rights in Heaven, I was also becoming introduced to my legal rights on earth. I learned to apply wisdom to every scenario we faced. My prayer targets were straightforward and consistent. I was determined to seek God for complete restoration, and I was not leaving prayer until I received the breakthrough.

1. I prayed for my son and I to be one in spirit even though we were apart. Spirit of Truth speak through us as we produce one sound.

2. I prayed against any demonic manipulators that would attempt to twist my son's tongue into confessing to crimes that weren't true.

3. I prayed for investigators to hear the cry of a mother's heart, not the anger I had against my ex-husband.

4. I prayed for a pure forgiving heart.

5. I prayed for my husband's good name and character to be re-established as God established it before the foundations of the earth.

6. I prayed for restoration in my family.

7. I prayed for my husband to continue loving me beyond comprehension because even I hated that my past was attacking him. I knew he had every right to be angry, yet I prayed for God to give him peace.

8. I prayed for the eyes of my husband. Lord, do not let the hurt distort his eyes beckon him to bring his burdens to you as he continues to love you and me.

9. I prayed for my enemies' language to be confused at the sound of God's footsteps in the courtroom.

10. I prayed for the safe return of my son.

A Warrior's Prayer Answered

One week later, I sat with the detective investigating the case. She said, "you and your son had separate interviews, yet both of your responses were identical. She interviewed my son at school a day before interviewing me. I had no access to him, not even at his school, and I couldn't talk to him on the phone. God was working it out. She then asked, Who is Charles Maris? I said, "That's my husband."

She said, "I don't understand why his name is in here. The Department of Human Services decided there's insufficient evidence that proves he did anything and he has full custody of his sons, is this correct?" I said, Yes, ma'am. She said, Mrs. Maris.... your ex-husband filed this report, and I am sorry to say this, but you're in the middle of a jealous heart. I am closing this case, Mrs. Maris. I cried right there because that was my husband's name, completely cleared. The battle wasn't over yet

One week later, we went to court, and surprisingly my ex-husband called my husband on the stand to testify against me. I was thinking to myself, how dumb is this! I knew I prayed for God to confuse my enemy's language, but it blew my mind to watch it unfold before me (Laughing). Yes, I know!!! His attorney called my husband to the stand to testify against me. They wanted him to be on the record, saying I was an abusive unfit parent.

The adversary had absolutely nothing to fight with because God rendered him powerless. I saw the verdict in Heaven manifest. God rebuked satan, and his plot was null and void. The judge dropped and dismissed all false allegations and charges. The case was closed, and the courts ruled in our favor. God rebuked the devour then gave me the healing virtue to help heal the heart of my son and my husband `through unconditional love. This was my first introduction to The Warrior Wife in partnership with God.

Women of God, we are Warrior Wives that stand with Heaven. We tally up the cost at every battle and wage war regarding our husband, home, and children in the spirit of God. Don't limit this book to a wife's earthly position because before the foundations of the earth; Christ called us his bride. This ranking of a wife supersedes the mindset that a woman has during any relationship's courting stages. This mentality is strategic, requiring discipline. It is the mentality of Christ that says, Exodus 23:22 But if you will listen carefully to his voice and do everything I say, I will be an enemy to your enemies and a foe to your foes.

CHAPTER THREE

The Warrior Wife &
Her First Love
LORD GOD OF SABAOTH

He is our dwelling place.

God is in the midst of us, and we will not fall. Psalm 46:5

The God of Angel Armies

Who is He to Her?

Let's get you acquainted with Lord God Sabaoth, The God Of Angel Armies. **Sabaoth** is the English transliteration derived from the Hebrew word **tsaba**. The book of Hebrews (2:10) calls Jesus Christ "the captain of [Israel's] salvation" — It is a title of Jehovah God's military might, His strength to fight and win battles. You may be asking how this title of God is different than just knowing him. Well, this is not a title; it is God's character. Many perish, lose battles, fight wrong because they do not know what is at their disposal. In chapter one, the life story I shared was an introduction to Lord Sabaoth and The Angelic Army. God gave me my own encounter just as he gave the men & women of the bible. Look at 2 Chronicles 14; King Asa had an army of 300,000 men from Judah and 280,000 from Benjamin, a total of 580,000 men. The opposer appears to attack him because of all the work he is doing for God. Asa was tearing down strongholds, bringing souls to repentance, the people of the land gave their lives back to God because of Asa's obedience, so the adversary (Zerah, the Ethiopian Cushite, was angry.)

Zerah had a vast army of a million men and three hundred chariots. Just do the math; the numbers did not add up. Let's face it, Zerah 's numbers would've slaughtered Asa's army because they were more advanced in weapons & skilled in battle. How many times does this happen? The numbers appear overwhelmingly greater on our opposers' side. However, the number one attack of the enemy is to make himself, his plot, and plan appear larger than the flesh can handle. Now Asa had a different mentality. He understood some things that his army did not. The bible said Asa put his men in formation, and before they clashed, he prayed. According to this prayer, Asa called on the name of God that is mighty in battle, and responds by sending his war angels.

Look at this prayer,

Then Asa called to the LORD his God and said, "LORD, there is no one like you to help the powerless against the mighty. Help us, LORD, our God, for we rely on you, and in your name, we have come against this vast army. LORD, you are our God; do not let mere mortals prevail against you."

- King Asa exalted and praised God before the verdict of the battle.

- King Asa recognized his weaknesses before God.

- King Asa expressed confidence in God's power.

- King Asa asked in faith and responded with a sure reliance on God.

- King Asa shared the entire situation with him, which is a depiction of trust and friendship. He knows God sees everything anyway, but he called God up as though he was on the phone with him or face to face sharing his heart.

- King Asa spoke from a kingdom citizen perspective. He knew he was a representative of God. He knew he was an ambassador, and he did not allow this battle to interfere with his identity. He told God if the adversary comes against me, he comes against you because you are me and I am you. I represent you, so don't let mere men prevail against you, the almighty God.

- Lastly, King Asa was reminding God of the covenant established between them.

Asa prayed, and God responded. Verse 12 says God struck down the Cushite before Asa and Judah, and they fled the scene. Look, God handled the problem supernaturally, but he did it before them, meaning in the presence of Asa and Judah. He wanted people to know they are my people, and to come against them is to come against me. God sent the future enemies a loud and clear message because the following scriptures say the other people were paralyzed with fear of God when they heard how God responded on behalf of these men. Do you realize what partnering with God means?

Lord Sabaoth will send his Angelic host to battle on your behalf, get the victory, so it gives him Glory and increases your faith to continue in obedience. Your relationship with God has benefits. Don't leave the benefits on the table simply because you haven't met this side of God. How can you know God if you don't get to know all sides and attributes of Him? For example, if the school calls me about our children, they get the role of mother. The school won't get who I am as a publisher. I may sound professional and can communicate

44

very well, but they won't know that side of me unless brought forth. The language of conversation is entirely different because I understand the call made to me is in demand for the mother (parent). Do you see where I am going with this?

Here is another example, I am LaDeidre Maris, Charles Maris's wife. We are pastors and counselors of Kingdom Maris Marriage Ministry. I have a lot of roles and gifts from God. If you saw me in operation as a wife, you would see it was different than my role as mother, publisher, counselor, or pastor. I am extremely passionate and protective regarding my husband; I am a warrior wife for real about him, but when I am ministering in dance or counseling, you don't see me in service to my husband. You know me in one area, but you don't know all sides of me. You don't know what I can do if you haven't experienced, heard about me, or encountered me in that area. Well, this is what I learned about God, Lord Sabaoth. I heard about God fighting on our behalf with angelic host, but I didn't understand how to pray for this level of protection. If you notice, when facing attacks, our free will has to be surrendered to God, which means I can't give God a piece of the battle and try to fix the other part myself.

I can't give it to God, then take it back. I can't give the battle over to God then doubt his abilities. In Joshua 5:13, The commander of the Lord's army appeared before him with his sword drawn in his hand. Joshua immediately asked, are you for our adversaries or us. He responded, "No, but as a commander of the army of the Lord, I have come now." Joshua asked," What does my Lord say to His servant."

Now Look,

The Commander of The Army of The Lord appears to Joshua holding a Sword. God's army has a commander that comes down and delivers messages on God's behalf. Not only that, but The commander also came armed, assessing the land and the obedience of the people. We can gather that our obedience to God plays a huge role in this level of angelic participation despite obstacles. We all are subject to God.

In Joshua 6:2, The Lord said to Joshua, See I have given Jericho into your hands, march around the city, all men of war; you shall go all around the city once, and you shall do this for six days. They couldn't shout, make any noise with their voice, nor could words proceed out of the mouth until the 7th day. On that day, they blew the trumpets while the people shouted. The walls fell.

We will face some tough battles in this life, and we can't fight with a carnal mind. We have weapons of mass destruction at our disposal. When someone decides to inflict evil upon you, it is essential to know your stance. God is ready to send his army into battle on your behalf, but you must know that he will use you to call it forth. When we reference God and call Him by name, He responds. Wouldn't you?

Let's say you're walking down the street, and someone calls your name. You will stop and look. When someone starts referring to your nickname name or a personalized name that describes who you are, you wouldn't even have to turn around, right? You will know that there are only a select few who know you intimately. Everyone will not call you by your nickname, so this must be someone you hold close. This is how God is. God is the same way. Where do you think you got it from? (in my country accent) We are in His image and after His likeness.

The bible gives us all of God's names, and every name reveals a side of his character. When we speak the name Lord of Host, we are releasing a war cry. This wail is different because we call for the War Angels of God to show up for battle on our behalf. The Warrior Wife and God have a partnership, which flourishes from trust and training. Please allow me to introduce some more of his handy work to help establish a bond between you two. You are God's chosen. When the adversary tried to come against God's Chosen, he was in for a rude awakening.

- Elisha prayed that God would strike the Syrians. Strike them with blindness. God struck them with blindness according to the Word of Elisha. 2nd kings 6:18

- Then the Lord rained down, burning sulfur (brimstone) and fire on Sodom and Gomorrah. Genesis 19:24

- He overthrew two cities, but he released Lot at the plea of Abraham. Genesis 19:29

- Moses told Israel, the Lord will fight for you, you need only to be still Exodus 14:14

- I am the Lord; I will bring you out from under the burdens of Egypt. I will rescue you from their bondage, and I will redeem you with an outstretched arm and with great judgments. Exodus 6:6

- When you are incapable of escaping the situation on your own—wait for God to move on your behalf Psalm 27:14.

- You will not need to fight in this battle. Stand firm, hold your position, and see the salvation of the LORD on your behalf, O Judah, and Jerusalem. Do not be afraid, and do not be dismayed. Tomorrow, go out against them, and the LORD will be with you. 2 Chronicles 20:17

- No man shall be able to stand before you all the days of your life. Just as I was with Moses, so I will be with you. I will not leave you or forsake you. Joshua 1:5

49

- The Lord threw their enemies into confusion before Israel, so Joshua and the Israelites defeated them. Joshua 10:10

- At Joshua's request, the sun stood still until they destroyed their enemies. The Lord fought for Israel Joshua 10:12

These are only a few scriptures regarding God's battles on behalf of his people. God is always in control. I do not care how treacherous or deceiving the attack may be. Satan cannot do any more than what is allowed by our God. We live in a fractured world. God does not want us deceived into thinking that we will never face persecution or hardship. We do not get to avoid the battles—in fact, 2nd timothy states that anyone who belongs to Christ will suffer persecution for his namesake. That means saddle up, prepare and be ready because the adversary is coming. Our Lord says I have told you these things so that in me you may have peace. In this world, you will have trouble; but take heart! I have overcome the world.

When a tormenting fear arises, the bible says perfect love casts out fear. God is our perfect love and to cast out is an action word. God will remove any spirit that seeks to torment. He will do it through us, which means we are to operate in our authority.

How is that trust developed?

Some trust in chariots and some in horses, but we trust in the name of the LORD our God. Psalm 20:7

1.) First, come unto him as you are, remove the thoughts about him that depicted him as someone in a cloud uninterested and detached from you. The bible says to fear God out of reverence for who he is because that is the beginning of wisdom.

2.) We need wisdom. Pray for wisdom and a heart to reverence God always. Reverence means having a deep respect and regard for him.

3.) Quiet your soul and talk to him like you would a friend sitting in front of you. Share your heart with him, cry out of your soul for him and unto him.

4.) Push everything away and make God a priority. He wants you and him to meet face to face in faith.

5.) Receive Jesus Christ as your Lord and Savior, know that he thought you were worth dying for so that he could live within. Galatians 2:20 It is no longer you who lives but Christ who lives in you. The life you now live in the flesh is lived by faith in the Son of God who loves you.

6.) Now ask to be filled with the power of the Holy Spirit. Every wife needs her partner, the Holy Spirit.

What does a partnership with God look like?

The Warrior Wife and God have their own secret place of meeting. For me, it is thru writing, spending time at the water, and prayer.

He is with me everywhere I go, but it is in these times that he and I consummate. There's a dialogue where we intertwine, and I lend my ear to hear. I submit to the transformation of the Lord because I need him.

I crave him more than life itself. He is my life. He is my reason for existing, and the love I have for my husband comes from this well in God. God is my oxygen, and before I can rise as a warrior, I must kneel as a servant. Even in my battles, I am still serving my God through worship, prayer, and fasting. I serve him in my obedience to his will. Absorb these three words…

GOD CHOSE ME…

God has accepted you as you are. The more you embrace God, the greater you become. Old things pass away, and behold; all things become new. God tells us in him we are new creations. Our partnership with him has little to do with our capabilities and more to do with our faith and God's capabilities thru us. Partnership with God is cooperation with the Holy Spirit. It is an alliance formed in the spirit birthed in the natural. Heaven doesn't 2nd guess whether they will show up for battle. We do that in our human nature and assume this is God's behavior. We second guess God. God knows what He predestined regarding your life before the foundations of the world. Heaven is a place of knowing, so we must know and not doubt.

Take one scripture, and just stand on that one scripture all week long! In order to know him, you must learn him; see him in action, and to see him in action, you must give him something, a situation, or dream that you are willing to take him at his word. This partnership is love and faith. It's been in the most challenging battles that I've had to stake everything on the God whom I love. Clinging to one scripture and holding on for dear life, as I held on to that Word from God, I heard God say.... The Government of God is within you.

CHAPTER FOUR

The Warrior Wife

HER AUTHORITY

And Asa cried out to the LORD his God, and said, "LORD, it is nothing for You to help, whether with many or with those who have no power; help us, O LORD our God, for we rest on You, and in Your name, we go against this multitude. O LORD, You are our God; do not let man prevail against You!" 2 Chronicles 14:11

The Authority of The Wife

Warrior, Release God's Power

God gave every wife a set of keys to unlock the hidden things of Heaven within their marriage. The adversary attempts to plant seeds of doubt within the mind, which causes the wife to question herself. The truth is, we have authority, according to Matthew 16:19. God said, I will give you the keys (authority) of the Kingdom of Heaven; and whatever you bind [forbid, declare to be improper and unlawful] on earth will be bound in Heaven. Whatever you loose [permit, declare lawful] on earth will have [already] been loosed in Heaven." Matthew 16:19 AMP. We have a special task here on earth, within our homes. As long as our words of authority and actions reflect God's will, they shall come to pass.

Have you ever paid close attention to your marriage license? Your marriage license is an earthly and heavenly decree. Now with all the rights and privileges, you have on earth concerning your husband... Why would you second guess your authority in Heaven? Now, Look down at your ring. Your ring on your finger is symbolic of your earthly covenant and heavenly covenant from God that never ends. We have power.

Jesus told us in Luke 10:19, "Behold, I give you the authority to trample on serpents, scorpions, and over all the power of the enemy, and nothing shall by any means hurt you."We must learn and understand our authority in marriage to petition the *Courts of Heaven* in faith regarding matters happening on earth. The authority spoken in Luke 10:19 is delegated power, much like the law enforcement possesses. When an officer steps out in front of traffic and holds up his hand to stop it, he's not stopping traffic with his strength – he is stopping them with the delegated authority that comes from wearing the uniform. The law backs the office. That's the authority we have in Christ. We are not stopping the forces of darkness that occur in our marriage by our strength – we are stopping them with the delegated authority given to us by God in Christ. Lord Sabaoth backs us. God Almighty is the power behind our authority! Ephesians 6:10 says, Be strong in the Lord and the power of His might.

Authority in Christ

Authority in Christ is not controlling or dominant. There is a difference between a strong warrior wife and a controlling wife. The description below will show two types of strength. The controlling and dominant woman is of flesh, pride, arrogance, & fear. She is weakened by her natural sight, so she only dictates, decides, and throws her voice at what she sees. She fears her past, so she tries to control her husband, constantly fixing him so he doesn't become what she knew. She is blinded by control because her past controls her.

The Warrior Wife is influential and influenced by the Holy Spirit. We are not strong due to controlling or dominating our husbands. The strength of the Lord is upon us. We know our heart in God, and we are the apple of God's eye. We know our posture in God, and because of this, we are an asset. We have value and influence, and we don't spew out unforgiveness in our homes. We are healing agents of change who don't have to take the credit for victories.

We want God glorified in all the earth. We are our husband's glory. We desire to see promises fulfilled all around us. We

59

have great courage and strength. We are nurturers, not self-promoters. We observe quietly and get instructions from God's perspective, not our own. We are free in our love because we received God's love.

Experiences have taught us to trust God beyond what we can see & comprehend, so we beckon for God to guide our hearts. We are not naive pushovers; we are uncompromising in God. We love extremely hard with no fear, and we are the wind beneath the arms of our husbands.

A controlling wife puts her husband down only to build herself up; she harms him down in his soul. While he cries internally, she performs for the public, wishing the show she puts on for others was absolute in her heart. She manipulates him with her fleshly attributes, and she has nothing of substance to offer. She refers to being real as speaking her heart when in actuality, she speaks from her carnality. Her husband suffers, and she talks about him to others. She compares him to others, weakens him, yet wonders why he cannot be great. So now she, the controlling wife, tries to fix him, and without God, she gives up. The reality is the controlling, manipulative wife is full of fear and insecurity. The Warrior Wife experiences fear, but we go to God and hide under the shadow of the almighty. As women, we have insecurities, but we find our freedom in God

Warrior's Declaration

The warrior wife cries in her alone time, but in the field of battle, she rolls up her sleeves to destroy the enemy for the sake of her family. No one, I mean no one, will ruin her family. God surrounds her like Zachariah 2:5. She closes her eyes, and she can see the angel armies of God all around her as she protects her family. She realizes her God is with her, and there is more with her than with them! She knows her rank in the spiritual realm.

So, she fights from that realm, a place of victory with the whole armor of God. She stands...stand with the belt of truth, stand with the breastplate of righteousness, stand with The shield of faith, stand with the helmet of salvation, and stand with the sword Of the spirit and fight... She is more aware of the spirit realm than she is the natural...she is the warrior wife.

CHAPTER FIVE

The Warrior Wife
HER ARMOR

Do not gloat over me, my enemy! Though I have fallen, I will rise. Though I sit in darkness, the LORD will be my light **Micah 7:8.**

The Warrior Wife

Dresses in

The Whole Armor of God

Armour of God

Wherefore take unto you the whole armour of God, that ye may be able to withstand in the evil day, and having done all, to stand (Ephesians 6:13 KJV).

Helmet of Salvation
(Ephesians 6:17)

Breastplate of Righteousness
(Ephesians 6:14)

Belt of Truth
(Ephesians 6:14)

Shield of Faith
(Ephesians 6:16)

Sword of the Spirit
(Ephesians 6:17)

Feet of Peace
(Ephesians 6:15)

A Chink in My Armor

Exposing Me only to Train Me

In the preface section, I shared my story with you, how I began walking into this mantle of The Warrior Wife. The adversary attacked our passion for restoring families unto God by attacking our marriage and family. He knew that if he could overtake us, he could get other families. The experience trained us for a completely different battle that qualifies us to teach others how to overcome.

God awakened a deliverance ministry within us. We learned the importance of knowing the strengths, weaknesses, and exposing our weaknesses to God. This section is not about Ephesians 6. It is about 2nd Corinthians 12:9. I will discuss shortcomings because praying for your husband without pushing your weaknesses into the presence of God is an invitation for backlash attacks. Jesus submitted his flesh through fasting and praying. This is what we must do because training as a warrior wife is different.

Warriors Train Differently

Warrior Wives train differently than other special forces in the body of Christ. What appears as chaos, distractions, and turmoil in your home is some form of training that will introduce you to the powerful bride you are in Christ. Each season of your life serves as a launching pad. I titled this section a chink in my armor because a warrior wife is also a vulnerable wife who understands she is strong, even in her weaknesses. The past taught us to hide our most vulnerable areas as though our weaknesses were defects. We separate ourselves from our insecurities because they cause us to feel crippled when these are the areas where the strength of God is evident.

Does Your Armor have a chink in it? Have you given your weaknesses to God? Lord Sabaoth has more than enough angels to release on your behalf to fight demonic spirits. I am going to share my transparent truth regarding the cost of hiding or being ashamed of flaws.

A chink refers to an area of weakness... I have liberty in Christ, so I am not concerned about being transparent. My only prayer is that my transparency encourages you. Please assess yours as well so you can begin to rest in God even during a crisis. We cannot put on half of our armor and still be successful. Covering in the armor of God means allowing God access to our imperfections

Chink In My Armor: Emotions

My emotions had a voice of their own. Sister, let me explain to you; I know what it feels like to have unchecked emotions leaning to their own understanding. Entering a battle with chaotic feelings causes your judgment, sight, and hearing to be impaired. There are times when my fleshly feelings sound like truth even though they are whispers from satan. They would cause me to panic when I needed to be at peace. I would be angry when I should walk in love, and I have screamed when I should have responded gently. Emotions without the Holy Spirit's direction are scary and will lead you to do your own will instead of God's will. I've learned to push my emotions into the presence of God daily, did you get that? I have to do this daily. The Warrior Wife needs her emotions; they are God-given gifts. Our emotions are also personalities of the Holy Spirit. The Holy Spirit gets grieved and quenched, those are emotions. According to scripture, our emotions must be aligned with Galatians 5:22. Emotions outside of the presence of God are chaos.

Galatians 5:16-24 ESV But I say, walk by the Spirit, and you will not gratify the desires of the flesh. For the desires of the flesh are against the Spirit, and the desires of the Spirit are against the flesh, for these are opposed to each other, to keep you from doing the things you want to do. But if you are led by the Spirit, you are not under the law. Now the works of the flesh are evident: sexual immorality, impurity, sensuality, idolatry, sorcery, enmity, strife, jealousy, fits of anger, rivalries, dissensions, divisions, ...

† Chink In My Armor: Thinking I'm Powerless

Sisters, my past mindset about myself has taken past conversations and created something completely different. The sword of God is the word of God. Imagine going into battle with either no sword, a dull sword, or a sword with no instruction on using it? Without scriptures, promises, truth, or revelations from God, the mind becomes a playground for satan. When we face opposition with concerns about what strategy or weapon to use, the opponent knows she is an easy prey because there's no discipline mentally. My sword of the spirit needed sharpening. I did not have enough of God's Word within me to fight my opposer. I viewed myself as powerless, which contradicts God's promises of reflecting him. People told me I had the authority, but I could not convince myself of this truth because my past didn't look like this truth. I knew Jesus died on the cross for me, but I had no biblical principles to fight off demonic activity, which meant that my sword of the spirit was ineffective. The bible says His Word is living and active, which means when I utilize God's Word, I have to believe it is alive and will do what it set out to do in the life of myself, my husband, and children. I needed to believe in my God-given authority and apply God's word; this helped my prayers be strategic.

Hebrews 4:12 ESV For the Word of God is living and active, sharper than any two-edged sword, piercing to the division of soul and of spirit, of joints and of marrow, and discerning the thoughts and intentions of the heart.

† Chink In The Armor: Unresolved hurt

Oh boy! I had a rough time forgiving myself for past decisions when I operated in immaturity, selfishness, pride, anger. I didn't have the breastplate of righteousness securely on, and thus my heart was left unguarded. When the heart is unguarded, anything can enter and take root. Unresolved issues festered within me, then evolved into resentment and unforgiveness even within our blended families among the co-parents. I would get so angry.

Imagine trying to fight spiritual wickedness in high places, and thoughts of something from your past, something your husband may have said or done, comes to memory. The memory triggers fear and anger, then disrupts your original plan to assist your spouse. The heart's eyes become tainted; instead of pools of love and compassion, the eyes become stained with anger, hate, and frustration. Confess that sin unto God. When we don't confess it, our adversary uses it against us.

Open arguments break out in homes when seeds of unforgiveness aren't uprooted. Guard your heart against evil attacks.

Proverbs 4:23 **ESV** *Keep your heart with all vigilance, for from it*

flow the springs of life.

† Chink In my Armor: My Mind and Mouth

Whew!! Ok, now I know I addressed my thoughts earlier, but this is a bit different because it's a combo. The mind and the mouth working together. Listen, there was a chink in my helmet of salvation. The Helmet of Salvation is not just about giving your life to Christ and moving forward. Philippians 2:12 says I am to work out my own salvation with fear and trembling, for it is God who works in me to will and to act to fulfill what pleases him. The helmet serves as protection for the head, and it is a vital piece of armor. An attack to the head could result in instant death. Well, what happens when the body begins to turn on itself. Sounds insane?

What happens when the mind and mouth of The Warrior Wife begin to speak negatively to herself and her spouse.

It starts in our thoughts then comes out of our mouths. Our minds are battlefields, and the outcomes of those battles determine the course of our lives. Romans 12:1–2 instructs us to renew our minds by allowing the truth of God's Word to wipe out anything contrary, such as old ideas, opinions, and worldly views. We must allow God's truth to continually wash away the world's filth, lies, and confusion from our minds and adopt God's perspective.

This weakness left unchecked can stifle your husband. The wrong words released into our husband's lives do more damage than satan could ever do on his own. I AM lives within us, and He created our husband from thoughts formed into words. I cry as I write this because I have failed in these areas more times than you can count. I have grieved the Holy Spirit; therefore, we can teach it because we have done it. I am God's voice in my husband's life, and he has always said, If my wife tells me, I can do it… I believe with my whole heart that I can. The husband was created to take the words of his wife and receive them as a decree legalized in court. If she says it, then it impacts him.

Every day I must check my armor and submit my weaknesses before God, so when I enter the battleground, He knows everything and equips me with what I need. You may not even know you have some issues, but specific scenarios will expose them. Address them as they arise. Take a moment, examine your armor, write down weaknesses and strengths, surrender them to God, and partner with Lord Sabaoth, the God of Angel Armies.

WEAKNESSES	STRENGTHS

Remember, there will be times where you will encounter spiritual warfare, which I call combat training. In the military, they refer to training as basic training. Basic training isn't to break the recruits. It is an intense experience that prepares recruits for all elements of service: physical, mental, and emotional. As warrior wives, we train on a day-to-day basis. Our afflictions and trials are not to break us; God creates and allows circumstances to occur that will not only reveal the true intent of our hearts but increases our faith in him. As we face uncertainties on earth, we must continue to rely on God and mature in God. Paul said, in 2 Corinthians, I pleaded with the Lord (3) times that this thorn in my flesh might depart from me. But God said, My grace is sufficient for you, My strength is made perfect in weakness. In these moments of weakness, we deem ourselves unworthy, unfit, not enough, and undervalued.

- What is your thorn?
- What is the one thing you need God to remove?

God will use thorns to let us see how he can take our weaknesses and still bring forth a victory.

CHAPTER SIX

The Warrior Wife
& HER HUSBAND

Is it your husband or a spirit you need to address?
Knowing the difference can help you learn how to address matters.
2 Corinthians 10:4 The weapons we fight with are not the
weapons of the world. On the contrary, they have divine power to
demolish strongholds.

Lord, Open My Eyes to See Him

See Him As God Sees

When Jesus said, "I do" during the marriage ceremony between himself (bridegroom) and you (church-bride); satan said, "I'll destroy it." He could not destroy the plans of God, so he set out on a different agenda. As you stood at the altar, the words of oneness left your lips, and you said, "I do." Heaven rejoiced while satan said, "that's ok, I'll destroy them instead." He set a different plan in motion that involved your husband. Travel with me into the spirit realm, please.... Your adversary showed up on your wedding day.

I know you were so happy that you had no idea he was present. Well, 1 Peter 5:8 makes it clear, Be on your guard and stay awake. Your enemy, the devil, is like a roaring lion, sneaking around to find someone to attack. The bible records that the adversary asks permission to sift you as wheat, which includes your marriage. He wasn't happy for you like everyone else attending your wedding. He's been watching your husband and studying his weaknesses. Trust me, my sister. He will not send your husband vanilla ice cream with

77

sprinkles knowing that he loves chocolate with strawberries. He is aware of his patterns, likes, and dislikes. Many choose to act as though he doesn't exist. However, satan exists. He is in the scriptures, and he attempts to hide underneath behaviors and responses. Where there is sin, he is present. Your adversary is out to get your husband's soul so he can frustrate your marriage and hinder you from fulfilling your purpose. Your husband has an assignment from God bigger than going to work, church or the gym every day.

If you are unaware of this, then there's your first mistake. Your opposer should not know more about your husband's assignment, vision, and weakness than you. Why? Because you have the Holy Spirit, and he is our advantage plan. He was there from the beginning in Heaven with the spirit of your beloved husband. If your husband has not received the Holy Spirit, pray for him to receive the Holy Spirit.

You cannot fight for your husband if you do not understand his partnership with Christ. In order to understand the call on his life, you must know the mantle of covenant that fell upon him. This mantle existed before he met you. The reason why God said, He who finds a wife finds a good thing and obtains favor from God is because your husband has the power to find, pursue, and cultivate. Just because he isn't operating in it right now does not mean the mantle isn't upon him. Pray for God's divine intervention.

The Mantle of Marriage

In the Garden of Eden, before Eve arrived, God Imparted Himself into Adam. He imparted the mantle of marriage.

Genesis 2:5-25 Message Version

- Transformation: verse 5-7
- Stability: verse 8-9
- Increase: verse 10-14
- Holy Spirit: verse 15
- Responsibility: verse 16-17
- Accountability: verse 18-20
- Companionship: verse 21-22
- Sacrifice: verse 23-25
- Holy Covenant (Oneness): verse 23-25 as well

God imparted himself in your husband before he formed you. He created your husband to reflect His marriage to the church in the earth, so he gave him some instructions. According to Ephesians 5:25, states, Husband, love your wife just as Christ also **loves** the church and **gave Himself** for her, that he might **sanctify** and **cleanse** her with the washing of water by the Word that He might **present** her to himself a glorious church, not having spot or wrinkle. **That she should be holy and without blemish.**

Everything in bold print is what Christ was assigned to do for all of us. Pray this scripture over your husband every day. This is called praying the will of God (the heart of God) concerning your husband. The husband is to walk in the footprints of Christ, with Christ, and in Christ.

The Mantle Of Marriage Prayer

Lord, I pray your mantle of covenant marriage upon my husband. Transform the heart of my husband. My husband is stable, responsible, and wise. Read the scriptures at the beginning of this chapter and pray them over your husband.

In faith, I speak boldly, saying my husband_____ (insert name) loves me as Christ loves the church and gave himself for her. My husband has a heart of sacrifice yielded to God and myself. He knows the Word of God, and he sanctifies me with it. The Lord washes me with His word through my husband, and he presents me to himself every day. He remains faithful to God and me. God and I satisfy my husband. We satisfy his soul, and he doesn't need any idol in his life to fill voids. When he looks at me, he sees love. We are the glorious church without a spot or wrinkle. We are holy. We are separated and sacred. In Heaven, we are seated in Christ. All my sins are on the cross, and I am without blemish. Thank you, Lord, for the great exchange between you and my husband. Open his heart to receive from you the mantle that belonged to him before the foundations of the earth.

Christ laid out the plan for your husband, and satan was furious with Christ for accomplishing this plan. Not only did Christ win and deliver us all from sin now he is raising men to do what he did for the bride. He is raising men to influence the church, teach, lead, provide, and raise boys to become like them.

Satan is furious with Christ and your Husband. *Satan was out to kill Christ from birth by using King Herod. How much more so do you think the attack will be on our husbands (see Matthew 2:13)* That's why we can't sit around and be idle.... We can't spend all our time trying to catch up with the latest trends and compete with one another. An adversary wants your husband, which means he wants you, your children, their children, and all affiliations. He wants to wreak havoc in your husband's life. Now, what happens if the adversary gains a foothold in his life. The next section, *Wounded Soldier*, will give insight into a delicate stage you may find your husband operating during your marriage.

CHAPTER SEVEN

Battling The Wrong Opponent
NO FATALITIES ON THE BATTLEFIELD

We have an adversary who is a spirit, and he needs a mouth & body to destroy your husband. Who do you think he will attempt to use first before he attempts to get your husband to self-destruct?

The Wounded Soldier

Scan The Terrain, Listen for His Cry

When God gave me this section, he wanted me to understand the internal wounds of my husband from the spiritual attacks of the adversary. I want to expose two different attacks that can occur and leave your husband (soldier) wounded. There are men of God that face persecution because of their moral, righteous stand for holiness, and then there are men who invite opposition into their lives because of their immoral decisions. Moral decisions are honest God-fearing decisions governed by God, and persecution finds the man who allows God to order his steps. Immoral decisions are ungodly selfish decisions that cause self-inflicted wounds.

As a wife, through your relationship with Christ, God will reveal your husband's condition so you may understand the nature of the attack. When God reveals the condition, you will know how to engage in warfare and fight for your marriage together.

This is not a section to support an abusive husband or the husband on a drug-related substance. Abuse can be physical, mental, or emotional. I must insert this disclaimer because I don't want any wife to read this and remain in anything that puts their life or children's lives in danger, thinking you can save him. If you are in a life-threatening marriage, please seek counsel.

Brokenness has no gender or preference. It will find the weak and the strong. Your husband is no exception. May I paint a scenario for you?

If you saw your husband with bloody bruises, a cast on his leg limping down the hall, you would feel compassion for him, right? You would feel the need to come to his aid and help him because you can visibly see his discomfort. What if you saw him bent over holding his stomach, trying to keep his entrails from falling out? You approach him to realize that he was slit open, and he is trying all by himself to keep this wound from getting worse. Would you be less abrasive and gentler in the way you cared for him? Could he count on you to protect him and get him to the right specialist that could stitch him, seal the wound, and help him heal?

The depiction above captures a wounded husband in the spirit realm. He is walking around fine in the natural, but certain things trigger his pain. It floods back into his mind and heart. He sits in this shell, shocked by the satanic blows he has endured over the years.

He is hanging on for dear life, all while whispering, I want to be respected and loved. The hurting husband is the husband whose wounds are not visible to the naked eye; his wounds are spiritual. The adversary's attacks have cut him wide open, and he's hanging there trying to be strong for you. He is trying to be a man, but it's difficult to be strong while suffering to death. The two do not make sense to him. He wants to protect you, yet he feels inadequate. He wants to hold you close and tell you he is scared. However, he feels insignificant in the sight of God and before you. The opposer caught him unguarded and beat him up either through his past, work, the children, or thru you, his wife. You are the one God sent to him, yet your adversary saw your weakness too. He turned your focus on yourself, and all you could see was what your husband wasn't doing.

How do I know?

I know because I was guilty of speaking inappropriately due to past fears; fear of being abandoned, fear of being controlled, and fear of being manipulated…. This is what you call battling the wrong opponent.

If someone told you that you were crushing your husband, you would immediately say, "That's absurd" I love God and my Husband. I wouldn't dare crush him because I don't destroy who God loves. Yet we have an adversary who is a spirit, and he needs a mouth & a body to dismantle your husband. Who do you think he will attempt to use first?

You are first on his list! Whether you know it or not, You are the bridge between your Husband and God because you are in Christ seated at the right hand of God. This is truly your position in the spirit realm; however, if you only see yourself as this little wife with no value, no power, bent over crying woe it's me, then you are the perfect candidate for satan to use to destroy your husband… Your opposer doesn't want you to know who you are in Christ, and he doesn't want you to tap into the greater intimacy between you and Christ.

Your strength is in your intimacy with Christ. Throughout the bible, Jesus heals many men, men that were crying out for help. He healed young and old there was no discrimination. Jesus recognized their cries. *In the book of Matthew 20:29-34, there is a story of two blind men. They were without vision. This has multiple meanings because there is natural blindness and spiritual blindness.*

The bible records that when these two men heard that Jesus was going by, they shouted, "Lord, Son of David, have mercy on us.!" The crowd rebuked them and told them to be quiet, but they shouted louder to get Jesus' attention. Jesus stopped and called them, "What do you want me to do for you?" The men answered and said We want our sight. Jesus had compassion on them and touched their eyes. They immediately received their sight and followed him.

In this recording, we see hurting men. The bible does not say they are husbands, but we need to see them as men with spiritual and natural defects. They had no vision or any direction of where to go in the future. They were stuck in the darkness, waiting for exposure to light. They were crying internally, and we can assume from their cry of desperation that they were in captivity inside their dysfunction.

The blind men were in bondage, and no one, not even the crowd, wanted to hear them cry. All those people told those two men to be silent. I can imagine people in the crowd thinking, stop whining... Be a man or just be the strong silent type. These people had no sympathy or compassion for their condition; No one cared enough to lead them into the arms of God almighty. These men were left to cry out for themselves. They were wounded soldiers trying to fight on a battlefield where they were already disadvantaged. As I studied this passage, God revealed the behavior of the crowd could take on any role. We can view the crowd as a wife ignoring the cries and concerns of her hurting husband. However, we choose to see this passage, one thing is evident. The man was broken, lonely, without sight, without friends, without love. He had no respect because people treated him like he was nothing. Everyone was ok with him functioning in his dysfunction.

EVERYONE EXCEPT JESUS ....

Their cries of desperation and shouting caught Jesus's attention which means it caught God's eye. God was receptive and responded with a question, "What do you want me to do for you." Jesus was sensitive to their needs, and he spoke directly to them. They expressed we are hurting, and we need you. God answered the cries....

The question that I raise to you is who are you in this passage?

The Crowd?   Or Jesus?

We must understand how valuable our role is in our husband's lives. We are in the image of Christ, seated in Christ, chosen to walk in Christ and release healing. There was healing in Jesus's touch. No one touches your husband more than you. Let your touch be sensitive on his heart. The words released from you should be so gentle that it shapes his soul. No one talks to him more than you. Some husbands are not hurting because he chooses to; he is hurting because his adversary has assigned different tormenting spirits to hinder him. Spirits are harassing your husband, and without God's eyes to see, it appears that he is angry all the time, frustrated, selfish, or emotionally unstable.

Your husband is hurting, and he is shouting within himself, asking for help. How can you be an armor bearer to others and your children, but you leave the leader unguarded?

Never under any circumstances do you leave the leader of your home unguarded. He is always the first into battle protecting you in the spirit realm, so do not leave him on the battlefield called life, especially if he shows signs of fatigue. Jehoshaphat in 2 chronicles 20:30 needed rest from battle. He won the battle but was tired from the war around him.

Men get hurt, and they get tired. Your husband needs you.

- If you are guilty of being the crowd, please repent. Don't rebuke your husband with scriptures when all he needs is your touch.
- If there's anyone who committed adultery against their husband. Repent for choosing someone else that appeared to be stronger and better. The behavior truly hurt him, and now he battles in his mind.
- Repent for breaking him when you didn't respect him even in his fragile state. He was and is still a man worthy of respect.
- Repent for giving in to the pain and giving up on him.
- Repent for fighting him. Some marriages have fought, and while they try to recover, the mental bruises always surface.

Jesus didn't destroy those two blind men. He built and led them. Once healed, they didn't return to their old sinful ways. The bible says they received their sight and followed Jesus. We influence our leaders and then follow God in them. Lead and influence are two different things. My Husband and I are two strong leaders, but that doesn't permit me to lead him as though I am head of the household. I can influence his soul into the presence of God, and I can conduct myself accordingly, as 1 Peter 3:1-2 states, Wives, in the same way, submit yourselves to your husbands so that, if any of them do not believe the word, they may be won over without words by the behavior of their wives,

The Warrior Wife doesn't see her own agenda and lean to her own understanding. The world says if you break a man with your mouth by telling him all that he isn't doing, then that's building him. It has this notion that if you point out his flaws, he will desire to do better. Yet, in the Kingdom of God, God does not break you where you are already broken. He restores you. The mindset in Heaven is I must heal you to build you. We must let the Holy Spirit train our eyes to see and hear the cries of the husband. I want to share my intimate writings with you that God shared with me.

God revealed this to me in my journal...

I looked deep into the eyes of my Husband one day after what we call "Heated Fellowship" (disagreement), and I saw this little boy curled up in a corner crying. He couldn't articulate his words or emotions like us women, so he was silently weeping.

In the natural, I saw my husband sitting in his favorite chair at home, but spiritually, I saw a little boy waiting to be held, waiting for someone to say don't be scared, or this pressure that you feel doesn't have to be carried alone. I saw a body of light walk over to him and hold him.

This light of God did something I couldn't do, or my pride thru anger wouldn't let me see what God saw down deep in his soul. God kissed my husband in places of his heart that I couldn't. He rubbed his head in ways that I couldn't, all while he respected and loved him. In God's eyes, we are all his children; there's no such thing as being all grown up. God didn't hold him hostage in his mistakes. He didn't hurt his feelings because he didn't complete a task correctly. He respected him because he created him to look and be just like him. They had this relationship that didn't require a lot of talking. God heard the whispers of his heart, and he listened to the cries in his arguments.

God was understanding towards him. He had compassion for him. God didn't see what I saw when I was angry with my husband. God showed me that my eyes in hurt are tainted.

When you look out of the eyes of pain, years of mistakes, unforgiveness, bitterness, resentment, you miss my eyesight altogether. He said, "This is my son in whom I am well pleased. I love my son." I realized that when God sees my husband, he sees Christ. He sees the blood that was slain and precious in his sight. God said, "I gave him to you, not for you to crucify him repeatedly. I am entrusting him with you, and I need you to see him as I see him. Respect him as I respect him. Love him as I love him, forgive him as I forgive him, and get to know him as I know him. Don't push him into a shell causing him to never communicate with you. Don't discard his words simply because they do not sound like yours. Do not bruise his ego because it feels good. His soul bears the scars of your words and your unforgiving ways." I sobbed, yet God said, "In your eyes, he's just a man, but in my eyes, He's everything to me. I gave up my only son for him so that he could live and be loved. Now follow my heart concerning him and be the armourbearer of his life."

At that moment, I cried and gave up my eyes for God's eyes. I learned something valuable. When I am hurting, I will only see my husband out of the eyes of hurt. I'll lash out with my mouth because of what's buried deep in my heart. We must examine ourselves hindrance to her husband. Satan loves the hurting wife. He knows her hurt gives him access to destroy herself and her husband...

You may be thinking, Well, I am hurting because of my husband. My answer to you is, No, you are hurting because of your adversary, and he may have used your husband to do it. You are his armor-bearer.

CHAPTER EIGHT

Warrior Wife Adjust Your Crown

ARMOR BEARER AND HIS ARMOR

An excellent wife is the crown of her husband Proverbs 12:4.

So when the decree made by the king is proclaimed throughout all his kingdom,

for it is vast, all women will give honor to their husbands,

high and low alike. Esther 1:20

The Armorbearer

Our Mandate

You are the armor-bearer for your husband. Becoming an armor bearer is an upsurge in spiritual ranking because it is shared authority. Armor bearers are chosen to assist high-ranking leaders. You may be thinking your husband is not a high-ranking leader. Yes, he is. Your husband's behavior may not match God's thoughts about him right now, but that doesn't mean what God wrote about him in Heaven isn't true. The war gets intense alongside the leader. In Old Testament times, kings selected certain officers to stand with them in combat and bear their armor.

An armor bearer is a person who carries the armor or weapons of a soldier, warrior, etc. The gifts of the armor-bearer serve in the life of whom they are assigned. We will use the teachings of David, an armor-bearer, to understand more about ourselves as protectors in the realm of the spirit. We will pull from a time in David's life where he was a shepherd boy tending sheep, became an armor bearer for Saul served Jonathon, and then became King.

We will use him to examine his heart, walk through scriptural lessons and become armor-bearers on behalf of our husbands.

1st Assignment

Ascension from the Low place to the High place

There is another son keeping the sheep. Samuel said to Jesse, "Send and bring him" 1 Samuel 16:11,12.

David was elevated in spirit before it manifested on earth because of his heart before God. How does this relate to you? Well, before the two of you married, there was a discussion about you regarding your husband. Despite how things may appear here on earth, you were chosen in spirit because of your heart. Many may envy you; they may think they can do a better job than you. However, it does not matter because you were the one God chose, just like David.

Your husband found you, and he found a good thing. Someone (Holy Spirit) within you made him realize he needed to spend the rest of his life with you. You are the one, and you don't have to compete with anyone else.

God chose David, not his brothers. God sent for you, and the position given to you is very prominent. David went from a low place in the fields protecting the sheep to a high office covering the king. This isn't just a change of status in the physical form of singleness to marriage. This is God entrusting you with more because of your faithfulness and commitment. An armor bearer doesn't betray like enemies; our loyalty sounds an alarm in the land and reflects the consistency and faithfulness of God. We are stable in God, and your husband's heart must safely trust you because he can be won over by your conduct in doing this.

2nd Assignment:
Be Authentic in God and Identify your Gifted Weapon

Saul said to his servants, provide me with a man who can play well and bring him to me. The son of Jesse is skillful in playing, a mighty man of valor, a man of war, prudent in speech, handsome, and the Lord is with him. 1 Samuel 16:17,18

David's gift gave God the glory, soothed the king, and defeated his enemies. Look, his gifted weapon was a triple threat. An armor bearer must identify the gifts/talents God has given. What do you have to offer him that can soothe him and prepare him to operate in the mantle of Christ? The same gift God gave you to soothe your husband is also the gift that can run demonic spirits a flight. David established a deeper connection with Saul by remaining true to himself. David was a skillful player of the harp, and his gift drove out demons.

- He didn't have an identity crisis.
- He wasn't comparing himself to the servants who had other talents.
- He operated in his realm given by God.
- He never tried to be anyone else, nor did he try to do anything else to capture the heart of his king.
- He was not a doormat allowing people to mistreat him.
- In later scriptures, you will even see David putting down his harp and picking up his sling.

Armor bearers carry weapons, and just as David, they protect the land even against giants. The secret is David really released faith, and the power of God behind his faith knocked out the giant. You thought it was the rock? The rock was symbolic for releasing faith.

God needed to use something released from David so Saul could see the value of having David close while still giving God the Glory. What is the weapon God has given you? Whether it is a harp or a rock, both of them still ran demons a flight in the correct season. Don't let people make you think you need a sword all the time. It's our obedience that gives us access. David became an armor bearer because he was authentic. As warrior wives, we must be true to ourselves. When your light shines in his life, God within you becomes a lamp to help him see.

3rd Assignment

- Affections and Intimacy from God

*1 Samuel 16:21 So David came to Saul and stood before him. Saul loved him very much, and David became his **armor-bearer.***

Your husband should breathe in your love from God. God poured himself upon David to draw Saul into him. God's presence created the need and fulfilled it. We should be so intimate with God that the love of God draws our husbands into God. David stood before Saul, and he loved him greatly.... Saul had just met David, so it wasn't years (time in a relationship) that brought this strong affection for David; it was the presence of God.

The Warrior Wife is more than a frontline fighter; she is a frontline lover. Her love builds trust between her and her husband, so he knows she will not turn. A wife who loves the Lord is worth far more than rubies. She alone is blessed and worthy to be praised because God is her source of love. When she connects with her husband, she helps him feel safe to rest while driving out evil spirits.

The presence of God soaked the heart, so anything he set out to do, God went before him. God goes before us as well because he is our difference.

CHAPTER NINE

Husband's Armor Of God

THE FIRE, THE PROMISE, THE DELIVERANCE

The Fire, The Promise, & The Deliverance

Power Up

Suit him up. What is your husband dressed in, in the spirit? I know your first thought is to discuss the armor of God found in Ephesians 6, but God gave me something else for armor. I want to use Daniel 3:16-28 Shadrach, Meshack, and Abednego for this section. They went into the battle (fiery furnace) wearing clothes and came out of the (battle) fiery furnace wearing a different covering, stronger and improved than before. Get this point.... nothing burned.

- What did their armor look like?
- What made God show up for them and cover these men in the fire?

Let's briefly take this apart!

Daniel 3:16-28 NLT

Shadrach, Meshach, and Abednego replied, "O Nebuchadnezzar, we do not need to defend ourselves before you. If we are thrown into the blazing furnace, the God whom we serve is able to save us. He will rescue us from your power, Your Majesty. But even if he doesn't, we want to make it clear to you, Your Majesty, that we will never serve your gods or worship the gold statue you have set up. "

Lord, my Husband, needs the armor of confidence, commitment, and conviction.

Remind him that he has a strong defense and rescue team. Give my husband, _____ (Insert Husband Name) courage to stand firm in his convictions from you. Grab the attention of his adversary by the powerful heavenly words that proceed from his mouth as he declares his unfailing love and commitment to you.

Nebuchadnezzar was so furious with Shadrach, Meshach, and Abednego that his face became distorted with rage. He commanded that the furnace be heated seven times hotter than usual. Then he ordered some of the strongest men of his army to bind Shadrach, Meshach, and Abednego and throw them into the blazing furnace. So, they tied them up and threw them into the furnace, fully dressed in their pants, turbans, robes, and other garments. And because the king, in his anger, had demanded such a hot fire in the furnace, the flames killed the soldiers as they threw the three men in.

Lord, my Husband,

needs the armor of faithfulness and devotion.

Instruct him to stand in the face of what appears to be an ambush from satan. I know you allow specific attacks to come against him, but I depend on you, God, to rise in him. Your promise says that if God is for him, then no one can be against him. Keep him steadfast and immoveable. Abound (securely be tied into) you. Keep his feet planted in your presence. When the adversary turns up the heat, decrease his fear by intensifying your love through me.

So, Shadrach, Meshach, and Abednego, securely tied, fell into the roaring flames. But suddenly, Nebuchadnezzar jumped up in amazement and exclaimed to his advisers, "Didn't we tie up three men and throw them into the furnace?" "Yes, Your Majesty, we certainly did," they replied. "Look!" Nebuchadnezzar shouted. "I see four men, unbound, walking around in the fire unharmed! And the fourth looks like a god!"

Lord, my husband needs the armor of your presence.

Let his enemies see you with him inside of the fire. Seal the gates and even as the temperature rises, blow on him, breathe in him. Let them see that he is surrounded by what seems like smoke, but it is the glory cloud. God, I need Heaven to hover around him. Save him, Lord, from the fowler's snare and the deadly pestilence. Be his refuge and his dwelling place, so when harm approaches him, it won't dare overtake him. No disaster will come near him.

Then Nebuchadnezzar came as close as he could to the door of the flaming furnace and shouted: "Shadrach, Meshach, and Abednego, servants of the Most High God, come out! Come here!" So, Shadrach, Meshach, and Abednego stepped out of the fire. Then the high officers, officials, governors, and advisers crowded around them and saw that the fire had not touched them. Not a hair on their heads was singed, and their clothing was not scorched. They did not even smell of smoke! Then Nebuchadnezzar said, "Praise to the God of Shadrach, Meshach, and Abednego! He sent his angel to rescue his servants, who trusted in him. They defied the king's command and were willing to die rather than serve or worship any god except their own God.

Lord, My Husband needs the
armor of sacrifice and evangelism.

I pray for his heart to sacrifice for you, and in this decision, he draws others to Christ. The people who were once enemies become the very people that give their souls to you, God.

My husband's life is a fountain of you, God, that draws souls to drink from the living well of your word.

Seal his Armor Lord

God,

I intercede on behalf of my husband _____ . Give him a heart of obedience to operate in his spiritual armor. Dress him in your spiritual clothing. Drape him in the whole armor of God from his head to his feet, Lord. Adorn him with your presence and give him a heart of submission so he will be able to resist evil. Gird his waist with truth, clothe him in integrity and position his breastplate of righteousness on him that no arrows of deception enter his heart.

God, guard his tongue so he doesn't and continue to lead him as you keep his feet ready, preparing to teach, preach, and spread your Gospel of peace. Let him walk in peace even when anxiety tries to tell him to worry. Give him the shield of faith so that he can quench the fiery darts of the wicked one. Take the helmet of salvation and place it upon his head. In his hands put the sword of the spirit and hide the bible in his heart. God, I trust my husband with you. Thank you for fully dressing him in your glory and strength. Now place your wall of fire around him in Jesus's Name.

112

Conclusion

Warrior Wife, who told you, you could not fight for your marriage? Who told you, you had no authority? Let me ask you this.... In life, if anything occurs with your husband, tell me who has the authority to make decisions on his behalf. You, right? You have full authority from Heaven to earth. Guess what? Earth's government received some insight from Heaven's government regarding marriage.

In the courts on earth, you and your husband are one. The wife has the authority to legislate on the husband's behalf because the decree says so. In the courts of Heaven, you, your husband, and Christ are one. The government within you is Jesus Christ. You are under the blood of Christ; you sound like Christ, and Christ loves and respects your husband. Now step in your God-given authority, legislate, and fight.

Made in the USA
Columbia, SC
06 June 2021